A World of Food

NIGERIA

Dereen Taylor

W
FRANKLIN WATTS

First published in paperback in 2015

First published in 2010 by Franklin Watts

Franklin Watts
338 Euston Road
London NW1 3BH

Franklin Watts Australia
Level 17/207 Kent Street, Sydney, NSW 2000

Produced by Arcturus Publishing Limited,
26/27 Bickels Yard, 151–153 Bermondsey Street, London SE1 3HA

Series concept: Alex Woolf
Editor: Alex Woolf
Designer: Jane Hawkins
Map illustrator: Stefan Chabluk
Picture researcher: Alex Woolf

Picture Credits
Alamy: 24 (Andrew Holt).
Corbis: cover and 4 (Gero Breloer/dpa), 7 (Paul Almasy), 8 (Paul Almasy), 9 (George Steinmetz), 11 (Howard Burditt/Reuters), 12 (Envision), 13 (Liba Taylor), 14 (Wolfgang Langenstrassen/dpa), 15 egg-fried plantains (Mallet/photocuisine), 16 (Paul Almasy), 17 (Homer Sykes), 18 (Ed Kashi), 22 (Onome Oghene/epa), 25 (Envision), 27 (Paul Almasy).
Getty Images: 3 and 23 (Tim Graham/The Image Bank), 10 (Nicola Peckett/AFP), 19 spiced boiled yams (Debi Treloar/StockFood Creative), 26 (W Robert Moore/National Geographic), 28 (Miles Willis).
Rex Features: 20 (Eye Ubiquitous).
Shutterstock: 6 (Vinicius Tupinamba), 15 plantains (pixshots), 15 eggs (Ray Torino), 15 salt (thumb), 15 groundnut oil (Marta Tobolova), 19 salt (James R T Bossert), 19 cinnamon (Elena Schweitzer), 19 garlic clove (Chernyanskiy Vladimir Alexandrovich), 19 butter (Kuttelvaserova), 21 balloonfish (Judex), 21 fish (Radu Razvan), 21 tomatoes (Pinchuk Alexey), 21 chilli peppers (Vakhrushev Pavel), 21 lemons (Maciej Mamro), 21 fish stew (Vladimir Mucibabic).
TopFoto: 29 (The Image Works).

A CIP catalogue record for this book is available from the British Library.

Dewey Decimal Classification Number: 394.1'2'09669

ISBN 978 1 4451 4486 3

Printed in China

Franklin Watts is a division of Hachette Children's Books, an Hachette UK company.
www.hachette.co.uk

SL001290UK
Supplier 29, Date 0315, Print run 4042

Contents

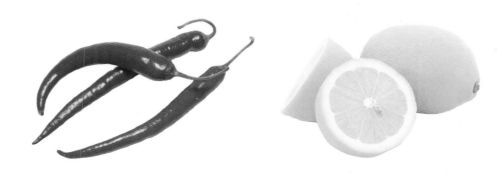

People and Food

Nigeria is situated on the south coast of West Africa and is just over twice the size of the US state of California. It has a population of nearly 150 million people. This is the largest population of any African country and it is increasing rapidly.

▲ A woman buys vegetables at a local market in the Nigerian capital city, Abuja.

Nigeria's population is made up of more than 250 ethnic groups, of which the Hausa in the north-west are the largest. Over 400 native languages are spoken in Nigeria. The official language, English, is widely spoken as a second language.

Place of contrasts

Nigeria has many different landscapes. There are tropical forests in the south and grass-covered plains in the central region. Further north is the edge of the sandy Sahel, a semi-arid region that borders the Sahara Desert.

Although Nigeria is mainly situated in the tropics, the climate across the country varies greatly. Southern Nigeria has four seasons and a higher rainfall than northern Nigeria, which has much less rain and only two seasons (see pages 8–9).

Cuisine

Nigeria has such a variety of people and cultures that it is impossible to pick just one national dish. Each area has its own regional favourite, influenced by the climate and landscape and the religions and customs of the people living there. However, most Nigerian meals are based around a serving of a local staple, which might be millet in the north and yams in the south, plus a spicy sauce or stew called a soup.

▼ A map showing Nigeria's key cities, lakes and rivers.

COMMON FOOD TERMS

Word	Meaning
buka	roadside stall
chinchin	fried pastries in strips
dodo	fried plantain
efo	soup or stew
fufu	thick, starchy porridge
gari	flour made from cassava
isi-ewu	goat-head pepper soup
iyan	pounded yams
moin moin	steamed bean cake
okro	okra
suya	roasted meat kebab

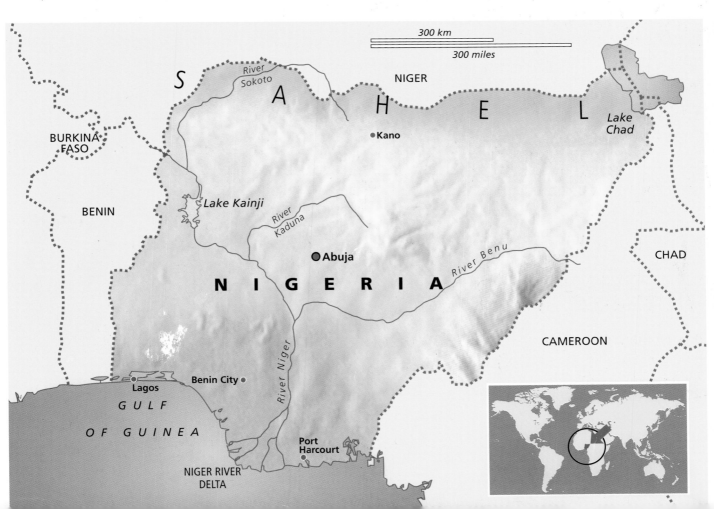

Before the trading of food and other products between different continents began, the main foods in West Africa included rice, lentils and the cereals sorghum and millet.

By the 16th century, European explorers had introduced various important new food staples to western Africa. These included beans and maize, which both arrived as a result of European trade journeys to South America.

Cassava

They also brought cassava, a firm, starchy root vegetable. Today, cassava is one of the main sources of carbohydrates in the world, providing food for over 500 million people. Africa is its largest centre of production. Cassava is perfectly suited to the tropical climate of southern Nigeria.

▲ Cassava can grow up to 80 centimetres in length.

West Africans grind the hard and starchy white flesh of the cassava to make a flour called *gari*, which is rich in carbohydrates and fibre. The Yoruba people of south-west and central Nigeria eat *gari* with local varieties of *okro* (the vegetable okra) and spinach in stews or soups. They also like to eat mashed cassava.

MAKING GARI

Cassava contains the potentially lethal poison, cyanide. This is removed during the cooking process. The large roots are peeled, washed and ground into a mash. The mash is soaked in water and squeezed dry several times. It is then roasted to make *gari*. *Gari* can be ground to make a fine flour or soaked in hot water to make a pastry called *eba*.

Spices

Nigerian food is famous for being very hot and spicy. Chilli peppers, originally brought over from South America, are used regularly to flavour dishes. There is also a distinctly Asian influence to be found in Nigerian cuisine. Cinnamon, pepper and nutmeg are all commonly used to flavour dishes. These seasonings were brought to West Africa by early European traders, from their trips to India.

▼ Two street vendors sell chilli peppers at an open air market in Kano, Nigeria.

Landscape and Climate

Nigeria has a richly varied landscape and climate, which can be split into three main bands. These run across the north, middle and south of the country.

The north is mainly flat, with large plains that stretch into the semi-arid Sahel bordering on the Sahara Desert. In the south a wide, dense tropical forest stretches inland from the coast for 150 kilometres.

In between these two regions lies the 'Middle Belt'. This is an area of grassy plains and wide valleys. The country's two main rivers, the Niger and the Benu, meet on the southern edge of the Middle Belt before flowing down to the coast.

Seasons

Although Nigeria is mainly situated in a tropical zone, different climates mirror the varied land regions. There are four seasons in the humid south: the long rainy season from March to July; the short dry season in August;

▼ A view of Kano in northern Nigeria, showing the flat, semi-arid landscape.

▲ Flooding is a common problem for families in the Niger River Delta. People often have to live with poor drainage and no electricity or sanitation.

the short rainy season from September to October; and the long dry season from late October to early March. Temperatures range from 21°C to 33°C.

In the north, there are only two seasons: the long dry season from October to May and the wet season from June to September. The north is also very hot, and daytime temperatures can reach 38°C.

YAMS

Yams are large tuberous root vegetables that are related to the sweet potato. They are ideally suited to the climate of West Africa, and Nigeria was the world's top producer of yams in 2005, producing 24.1 million tonnes.

Crops

Different crops are grown in each part of the country to suit the local climate. Crops grown in the drier north include sugar cane, wheat, groundnuts (peanuts) and cowpeas. Crops grown in the fertile Middle Belt include sorghum, millet, maize and sesame seeds. Crops grown in the south include cocoa, palm oil and yams.

Farming

Farming is the main economic activity in Nigeria, employing around 70 per cent of the population. However the country's farm production has not kept up with its rising population. This means that Nigeria is not self-sufficient in food and needs to import food from other countries to feed its people.

▲ A Nigerian agricultural expert (left) advises a farmer on his cassava crop in Oluwaseyi, Nigeria.

Nigerian farmers often plant a number of different crops in the same field. This practice, called intercropping, increases the yield and makes more efficient use of farming labour.

Regional differences

Many of the country's food crops are grown in the Middle Belt, on the fertile river plains. Most of Nigeria's cattle, sheep and goats are also raised in this central region. In the dry north, agriculture is only possible where land is artificially watered. In the south, the Niger River Delta (the triangular area of land by the river's mouth) contains highly fertile soil where cash crops such as cocoa, rubber and palm oil are grown to sell around the world.

Fishing is done along Nigeria's rivers, lakes and coastal waters. Fishermen in small boats using gourds and fishnet hoops largely fish for food for their families. Only 10 per cent of fishing is for commerce.

Farming families

Most farms are small, but with help from the government they are getting bigger and being run more efficiently. Families often live together in a family compound, with several generations living and working together to feed themselves. Most farming families are very poor. They often lack basic amenities and services, including clean water, electricity and roads.

STAPLE CROPS AND CASH CROPS

Staple crops are grown by farmers to feed their families. They include cassava, maize, rice, yams and beans. These foods form the basis of the Nigerian diet. Cash crops are grown by farmers to sell abroad. They include cocoa, rubber, cotton and palm oil.

▲ A Nigerian fisherman casts his net into a river near the south-eastern city of Port Harcourt.

Culinary Traditions

Many Nigerian families grow their own food. Because there is little running water and electricity in rural areas, it is usual for families to prepare food using traditional methods. Meals are often cooked outside over an open fire. Gas stoves are sometimes used, but the fuel is too expensive for many Nigerians to afford.

Typical meals

Although cooked food can be bought at roadside stalls called *buka*, most families eat their meals at home. It is part of the Nigerian culture for people to always cook extra food in case visitors drop by at mealtimes.

Most Nigerian meals are made up of one course. Nearly all dishes are based around a serving of a local staple such as rice or maize, plus a spicy soup. Many recipes have been passed down from one generation to the next.

▶ This Nigerian goat stew is served with okra, along with side dishes of fufu and plantains.

Fufu

Fufu is a staple food of West and Central Africa. It is a thick porridge, usually made by boiling starchy root vegetables such as cassava and yam in water and then pounding the resulting paste with a large stick until the right consistency is achieved.

▼ Pounding fufu in a large pestle and mortar is a physically demanding and time-consuming job.

In Nigeria, the fufu is white and sticky, and preparing it is a special tradition, respected by many Nigerian families. The traditional way of eating fufu is to wash your hands before taking a small ball of fufu in your right hand. You make a dent in the ball with your thumb and scoop up the stew or soup you are eating with the fufu ball. When the soup is finished, you eat the fufu itself. The ball is often not chewed but swallowed whole.

BREAD

One of the main foods in urban areas is bread. However, because most of the wheat used to make the bread has to be imported from abroad, it is too expensive for most families to buy.

Throughout the Day

Many Nigerians get up early and begin their day with a small meal. Breakfast dishes include rice and mangoes or stewed soybeans. D*odos*, which are fried plantains, are also a popular dish to start the day. They are seasoned with salt and served hot or cold.

▲ Nigerian children often help with the cooking. This boy is preparing a meal for the younger children in his village.

Lunch

Lunch is eaten early, sometimes around 11 am. Soups and stews are common lunchtime foods, often eaten with hands cupped like a spoon. In southern Nigeria, two favourite soups are *egusi* and palm-nut soup. E*gusi* is a spicy yellow soup made with meat, red chillies, shrimp and spinach. Palm-nut soup is a stew made with meat, chillies, tomatoes, onions and palm oil.

Moin moin is another popular lunchtime choice. It is a Nigerian steamed bean pudding made from a mixture of washed and peeled black-eyed beans, onions and fresh black pepper. Some people add salted or dried crayfish to their *moin moin*, while others add sardines, corned beef or sliced boiled eggs.

Supper

The evening meal is often similar to that eaten at lunch. For many families, lunch and evening meals are served on large communal plates. Young children may eat from a dish with their mother, but when they reach the age of seven or eight, the boys and girls are separated and meals are eaten with members of the same sex.

RECIPE: dodo oni-yeri
(egg-fried plantains)

Equipment
- peeler • knife • chopping board
- bowl • whisk • frying pan

Ingredients
- 2 ripe plantains
- 2 medium eggs
- salt • groundnut oil

Ask a grown-up to help you with the chopping and frying.

1 Wash, peel and cut the plantain into thin diagonal slices.

2 Break the eggs into a bowl, season with salt and whisk gently.

3 Heat the oil in a frying pan, dip the sliced plantain in the egg and shallow fry gently on both sides until brown.

4 Drain the fried plantains on kitchen paper and serve hot.

Food and Religion

The two main religions in Nigeria are Islam in the north of the country and Christianity in the south. Nearly half of Nigeria's population are Muslim. Around a third are Christian, with Protestant churches often mixing traditional beliefs with Christian ones. A minority of Nigerians follow traditional ancient tribal beliefs. These often involve animism, which is a belief in the existence of spirits in daily life.

▲ A group of children study the Quran at a Muslim school in Ibadan, Nigeria.

Dietary laws

The Islamic holy book, the Quran, tells Muslims what foods they can and can't eat. For example, pork is strictly forbidden. The Nigerian Muslim diet, as largely followed by

COLA NUTS

Cola nuts are native to West Africa. The nuts, which grow on tropical trees, have a bitter flavour and contain caffeine. They are chewed in many West African cultures and are often used in ceremonies and rituals as a gift to present to tribal chiefs and guests. The cola nut is particularly popular among African Muslims.

the Hausa people in the north, is based on beans, sorghum and brown rice. Muslims are not allowed alcohol but love to drink tea.

Ceremonial customs

Food and drink play a central role in the rituals of all Nigeria's religions. Occasions such as naming ceremonies, weddings and funerals would not be complete without participants sharing in a special meal.

The Igbo are a people of south-eastern Nigeria. At a traditional Igbo wedding, the bride presents her future husband with a cup of palm wine, known as *ngwo*. When the groom drinks the palm wine, he is symbolically accepting the woman into his family and they become man and wife. To celebrate the union, family and friends break and share cola nuts, known as *oji*. The Igbo believe that cola nuts bring peace and social harmony.

▶ The naming ceremony for a newborn is an old Yoruba tradition. Here, seven types of fruit are used to celebrate a baby girl on her eighth day.

Yam Festivals

Yam festivals take place across Africa at harvest time as a way of people giving thanks for the food they have. In Nigeria, the festivals take place at the beginning of August. Different peoples, including the Yoruba and Igbo, have similar celebrations to mark the end of one farming cycle and the beginning of another.

The New Yam Festival is one of the biggest Igbo festivals. On the last night before the festival, yams from the old year's harvest are thrown away. The New Year then begins with tasty, fresh yams.

Oldest first

Before the festival starts, the new yams are offered to the gods of the land in a ritual performed by the oldest man in the community. Prayers are given to the yam god, Ihejioku. The elder eats the first yam. Then the festivities begin, which include dances and a parade. Traditionally, only yam dishes are served at the festivals. Yams can be pounded, fried or boiled. A popular Igbo festival meal is *egusi* served with pounded yam. This thick soup is cooked with fish or meat and flavoured with watermelon seeds.

► These villagers are celebrating Funfu Ma Tie in the state of Finima, on the Atlantic coast of Nigeria.

Funfu Ma Tie

Nigerian harvest festivals celebrate not only the yam crop but many other important farming events. Funfu Ma Tie celebrates the break in the rainy season when villagers can harvest their crops and start fishing again.

RECIPE: isu
(spiced boiled yams)

Equipment
- large saucepan • colander • serving plate

Ingredients
- 1kg yams, peeled and thickly sliced
- 1/2 teaspoon salt • 1 clove garlic
- 1 teaspoon cinnamon
- 4 tablespoons melted butter
- cayenne pepper to taste

1 Place yams in large saucepan and add enough water to cover them.

2 Add salt, peeled garlic clove and cinnamon. Bring to the boil.

3 Reduce to medium heat and cook for 15–20 minutes, until tender.

4 Drain yams and remove garlic clove.

5 Place yams on a plate and drizzle melted butter over the top.

6 Sprinkle with a little cayenne pepper and serve.

Fishing Festival

The famous Argungu Fishing Festival is held every year in north-western Nigeria. This colourful festival is held during February or March to mark the end of the fishing season. Events include archery, wrestling and boxing, as well as dancing and music.

▲ The fishing competition is an exciting climax to the festival. Men and boys race into the Sokoto River to fish using traditional gourds and fishnet scoops.

The fishing festival began more than 400 years ago, and in recent years it has become a major cultural event enjoyed by tourists from around the world. In 2009, tourists from 21 different nations, including the United States and Britain, attended.

Rattles and drums

The festival ends with a magnificent fishing competition. Throughout the year, the fish along a 1.6-kilometre stretch of river are protected. Just before the competition is about to begin, local fishermen go out in their boats and beat drums and rattle gourds filled with seeds. The noise drives the fish back into the shallower waters.

The biggest fish

At the sound of a starting gun, hundreds of men and boys dash into the water, armed with large hollow gourds and fishnet scoops. A huge variety of fish are caught, from giant Nile

▲ A balloonfish.

perch to strange-looking balloonfish. The fishermen have just one hour to catch the biggest fish. The winner gains fame and a large cash prize.

Afterwards, locals and visiting tourists enjoy eating, singing and dancing into the night. And, of course, fish dishes are at the top of the menu!

RECIPE: obe eja tutu
(fish stew)

Equipment
- knife • chopping board • bowl • saucepan
- wooden spoon

Ingredients
- 1 large fresh fish (Nigerians prefer *obokun*, but halibut or skate are also suitable)
- 2 lemons • pinch of thyme, curry powder and salt
- 450g tomatoes • 1 large onion
- 225g chilli peppers • 190 ml groundnut oil
- 3 tablespoons tomato purée

Ask a grown-up to help you with the chopping.

1 Clean fish and cut into medium-sized pieces before rubbing with lemons.

2 Place fish in bowl and season with salt, thyme and curry. Leave for 15–20 minutes to absorb seasoning.

3 Chop tomatoes, onions and peppers.

4 Heat oil in pan, pour in chopped vegetables and cook slowly for 20 minutes.

5 Blend in tomato purée, add marinated pieces of fish and cook for 20 minutes, stirring gently.

Nigeria has many local festivals that date from long before the arrival of Islam and Christianity. These festivals are important community occasions and include events such as weddings, funerals and the investing of a new chief. They are a chance for people to sing, dance, masquerade and feast.

The Osun-Osogbo Sacred Grove Festival is held in south-west Nigeria and celebrates traditional animist beliefs. Families make sacrifices of chickens and rams and offer tokens of cola nuts to the spirit gods.

Engungun

The Yoruba of south-west and central Nigeria celebrate the Engungun festival to honour their ancestors. On the final day of the festival, a priest visits the shrine of the ancestors and offers animal sacrifices there.

▶ These Yoruba are bowing to an idol during the Osun-Osogbo Sacred Grove Festival.

ANIMAL SACRIFICE

Animal sacrifice plays a part in a number of Nigerian festivals, including Islamic ones. On Id ul-Adha, Muslims sacrifice a goat or sheep to remember the prophet Ibrahim's willingness to sacrifice his son, Isma'il, to God.

The animals' blood is poured on the shrine as part of the ritual. Afterwards, the sacrifices are collected and cooked for a magnificent feast for the whole community.

The Shango

The Shango is a Yoruba festival celebrating the god of thunder. For 20 days, sacrifices are made at the shrine of the god. On the final day, the priest is said to become possessed by the god and gain his magical powers. He delights the crowds as he eats fire and even swallows gunpowder. The priest then leads a lively procession to the local chief's palace where they feast on palm wine and roasted meat.

Ama

In the central region of Nigeria, the Edo hold a special festival called Ama, which celebrates the fertility of the soil. During the Ama festivities, the Edo feast on livestock, including goats, chickens and snails.

◄ A dancer in a colourful costume at a village festival in Nigeria.

North and East

Although a typical Nigerian meal includes a local staple plus a spicy soup, there are some distinctive regional variations.

▲ In the dry region of northern Nigeria it is more difficult to grow crops than in other parts of the country, so people farm cattle and eat beef. This boy from Kaduna is taking a herd of longhorn cattle to market.

Dishes of the north

People in the north, who are mostly Muslim, have a diet based on beans, sorghum, brown rice and beef. Traditional food of the Hausa people from this region includes *tuo shinkafa* (mashed rice grain) and *tuo masara* (mashed corn grain served with soup). Hausa also like to eat kebabs, which are chunks of roasted, skewered beef.

Tuwo, a cereal-based pudding with spicy soup, is very popular in the north. It can be made from maize, rice or millet and is served with beef and vegetables. Women of the Fula tribe carry jars of raw, sweet milk, which they sell on the streets. *Aksi fura do nono* is a dish of corn balls with yogurt made from this milk.

Eastern traditions

For the people from eastern Nigeria, cassava is the most important food. Other staples include dumplings, pumpkins and yams. *Gari*, the creamy flour made from cassava, is very popular served with meat and fish. Another traditional eastern dish is *isi-ewu*, a spicy soup made from chilli peppers and goat's head.

People living in cities can buy food from 'chop bars' and street vendors. They may purchase dishes such as *ukwaka*, a steamed pudding made from corn and ripe plantains, and *moin moin*, a steamed cake of ground, dried beans and fish. These dishes may be served with rice, cassava or yams.

SORGHUM

Sorghum is tolerant of heat and drought and is one of the major food grains grown and eaten in Nigeria. Sorghum flour is made by the traditional method of pounding the grain in a mortar and then winnowing. The flour is often used to make a stiff porridge flavoured with lemon juice called *tuwo*, which is served with vegetables.

▶ A popular Nigerian dish is plantain with yam fufu.

Central, West and South

The Yoruba people of south-western and central Nigeria traditionally eat the cassava-based *gari* with local varieties of the vegetables okra and spinach in soups. Pounded yam with *efo*, a tasty vegetable soup, is a very popular dish, which can be served with beef or fresh fish.

Peppers and chillies

Peppers and chillies are an important ingredient of much Nigerian cooking. Used alongside different spices, herbs and flavourings, and a splash of palm oil or groundnut oil, they create strongly flavoured and often very hot sauces and soups.

Peppers and chillies can also be chopped and served alongside a meal as a relish. Their significance to Yoruba cuisine is colourfully illustrated by the old Yoruba proverb: 'The man that eats no pepper is weak, pepper is the staff of life.'

▶ Yoruba women shop for peppers and other foods at a market in Ibadan, Nigeria.

Fish and seafood

Fish is very important to the Nigerian diet since it is one of only a few rich sources of protein. In the south, near the coast of the Gulf of Guinea, Nigerians enjoy eating seafood stews. These are made with fish, shrimp, crab and lobster and served with yams, rice and vegetables.

A popular way for coastal Nigerians to prepare fish is to soak it in a marinade of ginger, tomatoes and cayenne pepper. They then cook the fish in groundnut oil.

Ikokore is a spicy stew made with fish and yams, which is traditional in western regions. Like most Nigerian soups, it can be served with rice, yams, cassava and corn.

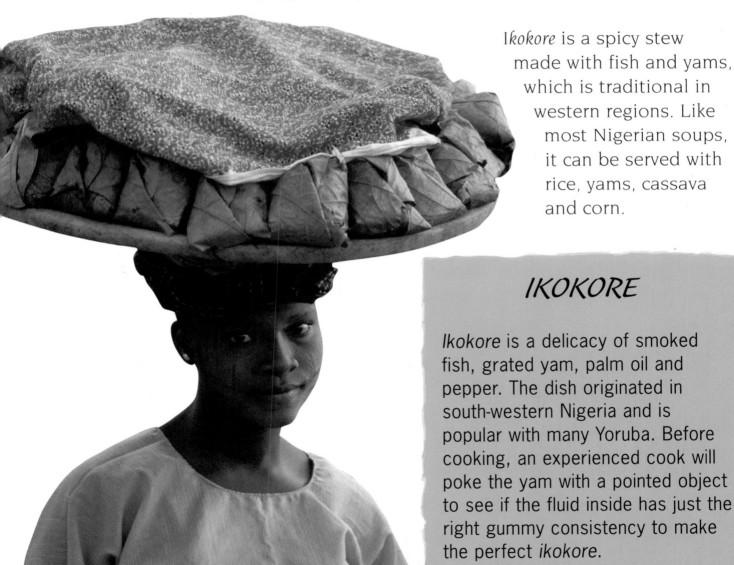

▼ A Yoruba woman carries a basket of food on her head.

IKOKORE

Ikokore is a delicacy of smoked fish, grated yam, palm oil and pepper. The dish originated in south-western Nigeria and is popular with many Yoruba. Before cooking, an experienced cook will poke the yam with a pointed object to see if the fluid inside has just the right gummy consistency to make the perfect *ikokore*.

Global Influences

As Nigerians have migrated around the world, and more Westerners have visited West Africa, traditional Nigerian dishes have become increasingly popular worldwide.

◀ This Nigerian chef cooks up some deep-fried dough balls during the Notting Hill Carnival in London, UK.

Visit your local supermarket and you will probably find a selection of West African staples, including yams and plantains. In larger Western cities, especially those where there is a sizeable West African community, you may find specialist African food shops and suppliers selling authentic Nigerian ingredients. There are also Nigerian restaurants where you can enjoy sampling traditional dishes.

JOLLOF RICE

There are many variations of *jollof* rice throughout West Africa. The rice is usually a reddish colour, from the tomatoes and chilli pepper used to flavour it. Then spices and seasonings including nutmeg, ginger, cumin and garlic can be added to flavour this popular dish. It is served with cooked meat, fish or vegetables either separate on the plate, or chopped and added into the rice.

Western foods

In Nigerian cities, Western foods, especially fast foods, are becoming very popular. It is not uncommon to find restaurants with menus that combine Western dishes, like an American-style burger, with traditional West African ones, such as *jollof* rice.

Healthy diet

So what can the rest of the world learn from Nigeria's approach to food and cooking? Firstly the West African diet is very healthy. Dishes based around a staple such as yam or rice, with meat and vegetables, are low in fat and refined sugar.

Few processed foods are used in Nigerian cooking and tooth decay and obesity are far less of a problem there than in other parts of the world. Also, the vast majority of African crops are grown organically, without the use of artificial fertilizers or pesticides.

▲ Students offer around samples of traditional Nigerian food to a class during Diversity Day at a school in Pflugerville, Texas, USA.

Visitors welcome!

Finally, and perhaps most importantly, Nigerian meals are very social, family occasions. Extra food is always cooked in case a passing visitor should stop by and be invited to join in.

Glossary

cash crops Crops grown mainly for sale in overseas markets.

climate The long-term weather in an area.

Edo A small tribe of people based in central Nigeria.

ethnic Belonging to a race or nation.

Fula Originally a nomadic tribe of herders who lived throughout West Africa. Some now live in northern Nigeria.

gourd A large tropical fruit with a very hard skin.

Hausa A tribe of mainly Muslim people living in northern Nigeria. The Hausa are the largest tribe in Nigeria.

Igbo A large tribe of people living in southern Nigera. They are also known as the Ibo.

import Bring products, resources or goods into a country.

intercropping Growing different crops in the same field, usually in alternate rows.

marinade A seasoned liquid in which foods are soaked before they are cooked.

masquerade A celebration at which masks are worn.

plains An extensive area of level, open land, often used for farming.

plantain A banana-like fruit that is cooked before eating.

population The people who live in a city, country or region.

ritual A religious ceremony that must be performed in a certain way.

rural Found or living in the countryside.

sacrifice The act of killing an animal as part of a religious ritual.

seasoning Something added to food for flavour.

self-sufficient Able to provide what is needed to survive without having to buy or borrow from others.

semi-arid With little rainfall and scrubby vegetation.

sorghum A cereal that grows in tropical climates.

staple A food that forms the basis of the diet of the people in a particular country or region.

tropics The part of the Earth's surface between the Tropic of Cancer and the Tropic of Capricorn. The tropics are characterized by a hot climate.

urban Found or living in a large town or city.

winnowing The act of separating a cereal's grain from the chaff (the grain's dry covering).

Yoruba A large tribe of people living in central and south-western Nigeria.

Further Information

Books

Country File: Nigeria by Ian Graham (Franklin Watts, 2004)

Fiesta! Nigeria by Tim Cooke (Franklin Watts, 2001)

Grace Kerry's Magic with Black-Eyed Beans and Other Recipes: A Nigerian Cook Book by Grace Kerry (Amazing Grace Publishers, 2004)

Lands, Peoples and Cultures: Nigeria, The Culture by Anne Rosenberg (Crabtree Publishing, 2000)

70 Traditional African Recipes by Rosamund Grant (Southwater, 2007)

Websites

www.foodbycountry.com/Kazakhstan-to-South-Africa/Nigeria.html
General information about Nigeria, and recipes.

www.motherlandnigeria.com/kidzone.html
Information about Nigeria, including a section on its food and drink.

www.onlinenigeria.com/recipes/recipes.asp
Some popular Nigerian recipes.

www.timeforkids.com/TFK/kids/hh/goplaces/main/0,28375,1044380,00.html
Simple facts about the geography and history of Nigeria.

Index

Page numbers in **bold** refer to pictures.